LOST AND LOCAL

LOST AND LOCAL

Poems

Carol Ellis

 **Pacific Coast** Poetry Series

An imprint of BEYOND BAROQUE BOOKS

Lost and Local

This book was published with the aid of a grant from The Lawrence
Lipton Trust

Pacific Coast Poetry Series
An imprint of Beyond Baroque Books
ISBN: 978-1-892184-26-9

Cover Design
Joanne Minerbi

Cover Art
Energy Crater #8
By Karrie Ross
Karrieross.com
2014 Copyright Karrie Ross

Beyond Baroque Literary/Arts Center

681 Venice Boulevard
Venice, CA, 90291

310-822-3006
www.beyondbaroque.org

Pacific Coast Poetry Series

Acknowledgments

Chapbooks
HELLO (Two Plum Press, 2018)
I Want a Job (Finishing Line Press, 2014)

Anthologies
Cloudbank Books: Just Now: 20 New Portland Poets, 2013, "Sidewalks,"
"Marsha," "Acupuncture."

Poems
Alehouse Review, "The Strange Mistakes of Fish."
Chest Journal, "Marsha," "Acupuncture."
Cider Press Review, "First Line," "Garden Snails and Bird."
Cloudbank, "How to Get to Germany."
Comstock Review, "In Every Building Something Happens."
Comstock Review, "Red Curtains."
Figure 1, "Returned," "Golden," "While Planting Fruit Trees"
(Pushcart Prize nominee).
Flock (Arq Press), "Hello," "The Only Fish of Its Kind."
Fog Machine, "Entry:," "Chekhov," "Roads."
Habitat Magazine, "a refugee moment."
Landfil (Ursus Americanus Press)l, "No Tomatoes."
Mojave River Review, "Shaking on Sunday."
Pacifica Literary Review, "Her Dance."
Panoplyzine, "The Walnut and the Rosemary."
Pomona Valley Review, 13, "Various Explanations."
San Pedro River Review, "Rough."
Saranac Review, "My Anna in America," "The Ceiling."
SLAB, "Heart Break."
Sobotka Literary Magazine, "Valentine Island."
SUSAN/The Journal, "The Chicken and the Cave," "Early Morning
Rosemary."
The Cincinnati Review, "Weathervane," "Stairscape."
The Syzygy Poetry Journal, "Sharp Mouth of the Cactus," "This Morning,
Listening from Her Bed."
The William and Mary Review, "Thunder."

Acknowledgments continued…

Tule Review, "The Ocean is Coming."
TXTOBJX, "Purple Notebook and Persimmons," "Fainting."
Unbroken Journal, "Fabric."
VoiceCatcher, "Current Conditions."
Wilderness House Literary Review, "Love Seat for Sale—$75 OBO,"
"Yellow Birds," "Wild Mustard."
ZYZZYVA, "Leaving Portland."

To Peter Sears, former Poet Laureate of Oregon

We are guided by roses, the scent of a page.

— Patti Smith, *M Train*

Contents

Lost and Local

Purple Notebooks and Persimmons

Filled with the year so far, addresses, names, the hard, the impossible, a list of groceries still waiting, notes for a book about leaving, this purple notebook almost left behind but found in time to be thrown into the car, on top of clothes from the last closet, the closet door opened quickly as quickly as a mouth gasps open, or wraps itself around the hill and valley of a spoon, or grasps a prayer please please before the spoon lifts, the hand shakes, the curious brain whose near-sighted and afraid eyes read words in the notebook on the table at the new house, while the mug of tea leaves a wet circle of *O* that will stain the purple notebook now away from the table, now on a shelf near the front door then orange persimmons on my porch in the morning and the young dog stares at me unable to turn away.

The Only Fish of Its Kind

In the waiting room with the blue plastic chairs and the yellow walls in the auto body shop where my car needs a lot of *new* and always the spinning grind of drills same as when I sat in the one car-detached garage in Michigan and watched Ed try to put a car together. I was in love. That's what mattered. A tall man—nothing lasted. Eventually I drove a 1984 Chevy Camaro red with a long gold stripe, the trash of my life wailing in the back seat across country to California where I wept between oranges and the ocean. Certainly there is partial recovery, certainly there is glory in this auto body shop and always polite waiting. They have my car, but the large tank is swimming with small golden fish. One looks at me or so I like to think. At this late stage nothing left to do but drive my blue car to a house lacking fish except in the freezer that's long gone.

Current Conditions

Their front yard fence with a rabbit hutch and a chain link fence
and rabbits running from my dogs on leash walking past because

even Alice in Wonderland worked with a rabbit
who was always late—held a watch pointing that out— especially
to Alice who cared. I had an aunt

named Alice—her nickname was Stormy— reflecting the
independent streak her family hated—besides she wore too much
makeup

and drove men into thinking about Ava Gardner
and other wild women who pleased them—their breasts and hips
easy enough to reach for—Stormy's smile

showed teeth and lips red lipsticked into commission. I watch a
movie old enough to be my mother and see a man take out a white
handkerchief from his pocket

and wipe the kiss marks off his face and hope none was on his
collar—the women wore white gloves— white gloves and their
many fingers touching

his arm then his face—someone is saying goodbye— leaving for
war probably—the man in a uniform ready for blood—the man
himself—hi soldier says a passerby

passenger—no answer—what's there to say when love leaps
away—that grey rabbit over there leaping.
Sometimes I take a pair of white gloves out

of a drawer and wear them around a few rooms— then take them
off—slide them back in the drawer— stare at them and the life
they promised.

5

Frog Chuckle

Frogs chuckle in the mountains –
fish wash themselves in the water I drink and swallow
all memories of water where I love a white sail,
one wing still flying in an old movie
as the pilot of a war plane struggles to keep
it steady going down after losing a wing to bullets.

Years later the children enter politics in the country
that almost destroyed itself and you –
but the white sail sails down a river
whose bridges I cross when I try to find my way.

But what can be said about brain damage
except that it damages?
Even standing up straight challenges
the trunk of me that could be a tree will be a tree,
roots down branches up sky rivers and the end of thinking.

I try to think more now on the brief ground remaining,
allowed. Pray for mercy.
Gather nerve as flowers are gathered
near the chuckling frogs and the hard ache
of a tall bird come to swallow them.

Basically Celery

I can't find the other hearts of celery and am in a raw frenzy—my craving for celery never before having been so profound—did it leap from my car when I stopped to have two house keys made because I changed the front door lock and the front door recently now I have to figure out where to hide the key outside on that off chance that I forget my keys that I forget where I am who I am why did life turn out this way and not that way as I said to my ex-husband when we were not yet married—this was our first day of talking—I said when he walked me down to my commuter train—when the orchards bloomed and never what has been lost been so lovely—you go that way and I'll go this way—and we did years later when it felt too late to go anywhere except apart—how did I happen to lose two dollars this week, first the dollar-off coupon then the celery hearts that I better not come upon years later as I am packing to leave and I lived through change, until change became a habit, somewhere to go when everything came at me dangerous, the dropped dollars, sanity to insanity then safe return for a few minutes until the lost celery hearts are all hearts lost, but there will always be someone looking for love.

Garden Snails and Bird

Two early morning snails curled together breathing each last wet breath. Their escape from wet grass become impossible they drown around their shells touching in love with the ground keeping them afloat their voices swimming saying hold me this one last time we leave together not alone our shells beautiful ready to be emptied of who we were come closer let my antennae touch yours while we say that we felt each leaf each rose in brief color scent have you gone already tucked into your shell your face disappearing the memory of your heart beating me into the ground as you rise above in the beak of a bird.

The bird is the word between us. Fly, do not wait to walk make the rhythm of wings beat your passion into airborne position flight is sight seeing itself see look over there look here answer the best question by asking even a better question who needs these dreary answers these complicated dances when a leap would do as well talking to you from the beak of a bird hoping, my love, you can hear me say love is the best moment when you slid under me a tenuous world opened you saw the bird first but I was already gone my head bowing toward your beauty as I rose above you only to smile at what had been.

In Every Building Something Happens

Bach drinks coffee over at a table for one
by the window in the café
where the rain outside shines

the streets until they glow from random light
from intentional light from light born today
from light falling into the sea

although a woman at the door gets her coat on
and then a hat finally gloves she is ready
to go out there look at her looking then leaving

already a block away closer to the bookstore
where she will touch what she has never read
these strangers on shelves she would kiss

the paper but any moisture
and certainly a rainfall
would dampen all past words

into smeared refusals to be read
the pages already out of the storm
and drying on the backs of chairs

Bach over there with another cup of coffee
hears what music only Bach hears
what sounds listen to other sounds sent flying

out of his head and when she hums
when she hears him hum they hum
together and what she hears is hers.

Divina Comedia

Then she walks down the street in yet another town to the bookstore where she surprises herself by sitting for a good two hours reading, remembering Dante and those words of his that always brought her close. Confessional that dark wood, lost, long ago he was, but close now as if he stood beside her and, like her, wondering again where she stands beside him. The bookstore a question of shelves and selves, the names dropping away from the titles that help themselves to the taste of content lost in remembered context, just a memory wanting change.

She walks through this dark city the way she imagines he must have walked through dark woods, lost, but finding himself there as she is now, starting over after a steep fall, as if someone picked her and held her up to the stars, let her know starlight—the strange close need of far away—try to climb out or stay in—but falling down down farther until she warms near fire burning with the many words for flame and the scream from flames embrace—until it is either lift or be gone into the bright burning story—show her mortal beginning, then the stone pushed aside the body gone far, far gone.

Look here, on her walk she sees a man sitting on the sidewalk with his cat, both of them asking for kindness, she opens her heart and gives because that would be what Dante wanted long ago and that man and his cat joins them in the dark wood, but maybe, even in another storm, even if it continues storming, the water will float her to the top, either that, or drown her. The new is always some kind of greeting. With a dollar she pays the fear off. The mystery begins again in the dark. She learns to never know, to love again the talking try of words.

Chekhov

Seagulls in cherry trees are themselves an orchard of sea birds come to land come to eat cherries the trees laden with cherries and birds and on the steps a man sits with his dog pulled close against his side but looking elsewhere.

The home not yet taken away into words the woman returned not yet drinking her hot coffee on this unusually hot day the last perhaps before the cooler weather chills the sorrow of empty trees and whatever is said before something is said.

Everything to say about wine red cherries in a bowl between us and the sound of his voice asks about flying the tall yearn of camellias the dogs barking at what in the next room where there is paper and pen the memories of a conversation.

A conversation that on some days will not stop talking about whatever we will not stop hearing. I listen and hear my father's voice coming from the margins of these pages – look like snow feel like ice.

He always looked unsmiling straight into the camera. He wrote his world. I read his world. My father rides a sleigh over the text where it is too cold to be awake in this room empty of anyone not on paper.

Various Explanations

Various explanations today
why a moth rushes a flame

or a fly's buzzing dives
toward a lightbulb

on because a woman needs
to read and think in a book

this book of poems
from a woman

the excitement between us
that the fly interrupts

as it seems to want my head
as if all her words

make my head glow
I am lit and loving it.

No Tomatoes

Rainfall and I am outside
in rain with rain as rain

apologies to everyone
to myself with wet hands

thank what air to look like that
I grow and comb my hair today.

Mayonnaise

I smiled at a woman walking down the produce aisle
and she smiled at me then slipped on a tablespoon
of dropped mayonnaise and snapped her left knee.

This was in Texas where I had just turned away
from the tomatoes otherwise I was surrounded
by lettuce and plenty of grapes one aisle over.

Someone warned me about the mayonnaise
when I walked in so I sidestepped it
its power come to be understood.

I knelt over her until she asked me to stop talking
her trip was ruined and I stopped talking
except I wonder if she ever traveled if she ever healed.

The Walnut and the Rosemary

I've been studying the think and feel of the human brain.
The large walnut muscle with god inside.

There's a walnut tree growing up against my house
giving the neighbors something to fuss about.

In about twenty years that's going to cause
you problems, they say, looking serious and tall.

Maybe you'll get lucky and have walnuts
says the man across the street who grows tomatoes.

I have a walnut growing another thought
that is if the squirrels don't get it.

A walnut shell already in the back yard
already too empty as a shell might be empty.

Today I bought a radio and two rosemary bushes.
Turned on the radio, listened, put the plants on the ground

Until I find the shovel and the strength
to feel my thought of digging and fill.

Brain in the Torn Left Pocket

Brain in the torn left pocket
shredded, going to far places unknown, unspoken,
rushing from thought, from the very thought of thought,
leaving skull fractured from thinking,
planning the end of plans
plans that knew pleasure never happening
happening pain abused words all gone wrong
a plaid flannel shirt ripped off thrown down
worn wrong all wrong
worth nothing going nowhere
brain in the torn left pocket
life never making sense of living
but living until now
the great ending finished finally smiling
at the lack of wonder
that made the head ache for more
until less was to wear
and nothing was to think.

Her Dance

The stage is empty. The floor is quiet as the dancer's face her face the dream of the dry fountain she walks past in the morning. The fountain dances water with a tall laugh and in her dream she throws a coin into the pool. Wishes living at the bottom of the world where she throws another coin wish when the coin taps bottom she hears her shoes tap the floor of the stage. Each step walks her further out of her dream into her dream of dancing of wearing a black dress a white flower blooms a gardenia already she stamps the stage claps her hands applauds in time to the music a musician sits at a piano stares at the white keys the black keys hears unwritten music keep its secrets she listens until she is her own one woman circle she dances the smile she smiles when she sleeps.

Early Morning Rosemary

This second morning of me lifting a possum not playing dead into a bag using another bag to touch lift—light light—and into the trash bin go both bags holding what they hold before the trash trucks take their screech and holler up and down the street this second morning of seeing a dead possum on my patio. Last night the crazed hissing at my dog barking until I went out with a flashlight and lifted the dog who slept all night beside me. Yet every morning a sign, an omen, a prediction—two in two subsequent days of adding a new challenge to my tone of voice steady lifting any time of day into the new rosemary bushes I bought at the farmers market and now have three mint plants that, in about two years, will make a man say "there's such a thing as too much mint" before he disappears.

First Parrot

He was new to me and I to him so we could fall in love dropping the history of old mistakes loving him loving the new the lack of memory the forgetting all that had gone wrong or right because he knew about the book with the drawing in bright colors that said *live live* with the parrot on the front cover we looked for wine but found only water in canning jars their rims suggestive of lips coming to kiss with each drink and were able to laugh about this new vintage this the first time together when I woke wild awake into not knowing that he would leave soon and take his stories about fixing broken cars in broken garages with tools foreign to my touch but he knew and looked at me when he read aloud until he was out of breath and stopped and both of us out of breath satisfied that we forgot whatever needed to be forgotten to see only the parrot's bright colors and hear it say the words of our names.

Brujas

Leaving the theater I stand outside in a dark

of black lipstick the world wears when everyone

leaves. The doors lock and there is only the makeup

of the dead and now I am past feeling

anger and cold while the bus continues to be late

and beaten memories beat me up until pain says

all the lines and I am down on the ground.

My body takes breath after breath as waves roll in

roll out behind the seawall in Havana where I walked,

the witches following me taking my hat

giving me one of theirs when to exchange is to continue

even with no intention of continuing but

what have I done? Left my heart in Cuba where muscle

beats to the drums of witches dancing

and will not stop until I love what a witch loves.

a refugee moment

you sit in your boat long enough but forget drowning it is where I
am made of moon and wind and water to shore sandy beach and
magical appearance where rocks melt and it rains until every
boat out there is an ark an invitation.

you are what swimming is as necessary travel but what country
loves you instead to let you walk into your life carrying your
story closely as wind the constant unexpected dream that makes
for two of you coming aboard.

How to Get to Germany

Slowly and remembering. Remembering my mother leaving. The importance of leaving. Of leaving Syria. Of leaving the moon and that star. Of leaving you. Of arriving here. Someplace whose name is a small white cup. An apple. An oak. I lean against you and swallow. There is chocolate and almonds. I have found three free chairs at the curb to put in my yard. Although I missed the advertised red couch that was also free. Everything is free and not free. I arrive at the border of myself. Here I am crossing. Where I left is another memory. It is salt. It is onion. It is a bitter floor. Here a ball falls out of a tree. The dogs are uninterested. I pick the ball up and throw wild but the batter swings and misses. The score is even. The boat is over there. My mother sits and takes the first wave out to sea. Her country is mine in wet dismissive time.

Then strangely the old clock in the room with no couch chimes three. Somewhere it is three o'clock and the clock is telling a story about three people who left the world. You knew them and refused to fix their screen door so they always had flies in summer. How angry they were. Blamed you for any insect that crossed into their home. That bastard. And surely you were with your long dark hair and cigarette. I could only fit one chair into my car. The others I walked home. One chair sits on my front porch that is small and rectangular. Not square. Only the sky is square and cellophane over candy. My mother's favorite. Hard candy those almonds. She came close to breaking her teeth in the chatter of chewing. But she is somewhere on a boat arriving soon. Although there is some land travel lifting her into the air that digs and walks her through time.

Postwar Detroit

When I was four years old
Vera put paprika on my eggs
to teach me Hungarian values
in postwar Detroit.

She was a refugee,
I was a postwar baby.
She learned English
as her second language,
I learned it as my first.

We both had family who disappeared
off the streets of Vienna.

My grandfather, the architect,
returned to Russia
only to send a coded note
to my mother and grandmother
that said, "Go to America."

In Detroit, I was interested
in avoiding garbage trucks
moving with the ferocity of tanks.

I drove a tricycle then,
and heard every day
the names of the dead.

Fainting

As I faint I remember my grandmother fainting onto the kitchen floor in Palo Alto. I brought a chair. I pulled her up and she sat as the queen of her own head's country.

As I faint I remember nothing of this. Only when I awoke did I know what nothing called out to her, her first name, my middle. Once in the Detroit basement together nobody fainting and she told me a story.

Although I couldn't imagine her young, suddenly deaf from a bomb falling near her summerhouse. The Black Sea caught slapping her beach of silence that held her when she fell in the kitchen.

The fall I hear when I fall outside for the first time falling nowhere near the catch of her arms.

I Want a Job

Suddenly with the quick gasp of dead relatives who look at me from photographs there of a marching band in Zurich marching past my parents my father has a camera and in 1980 he is on sabbatical where he researches the ache of protein in outer space and photographs what he wants to recollect. I recollect a photograph in my grandmother's room of her family my family—notice the distance among us—a family that did not work out, does not work out, does not work—I should be teaching—I should be standing among schoolchildren—we might be laughing—now it is 2 in the afternoon and I wait for the mail—those threatening letters to the poor.

I am tired of eating—chew on my tongue. My mother glares at me from the Ile de France that ship taking her to America, angry about leaving Austria lucky she did in 1938 got my grandmother out in 1939 and that's all except for Vera and Mischa who was a pianist with the Detroit Symphony—my mother was a social worker—at any moment I may rant or cry or make telephone calls to the man who lives on the roof.

My Anna in America

Freight cars passenger cars move on narrow tracks up to where her body lies her head thrust on metal ready to be crushed by love by transportation she won't live but if she did she'll live as a betrayed brain who never knows which direction she's going north south east west she's always there and breaks where she's been not where she's going until she looks at the words on her ticket where she remains a lost bag on the bench beside the balalaika player who hears the train plays in tune while glancing up now and then from his strings strum tracks to see her wait to begin that brave lie down crush down her eyes unsteady buttered bread waiting for the next smoked meat to be a meal for those sounds people make when they take a bite of someone else's life vitality gone flat on the bed the brain pieces collected into an appropriate simulation of her loving especially when properly combined with the good manners of fidelity and a train on time.

Last night she walked barefoot on the rocks scattered around tracks her dog held under her left arm against her left hip the rocks sharp but her feet never bled or hurt that much tender soul always choosing vegetables through the damn of hearing that tomatoes sob when stabbed by nails jesus christ how did he stand it oh he's come he's coming who knows even with him inside and beginning to pull away she does not know no deity's daughter just another woman rushing to catch the train and remove her brain from thinking about any of them of it of here she returns confused again about where here is and what history that old house lived before the gas station dug in next door and were there horses and who stood on the balcony and a woman on the front balcony waves as she jumps into my mind and knows I sit in my car waiting for the light to change to green means go, look everywhere.

The Book of Dad

Once I told him I was lonely and he said he never was lonely because he had the company of books. I read because I need the company—when the library opens at noon on Sunday a line of people wait to walk inside. In Berkeley down on Grove Street, I walked with my father to see those objects known as books. He held my hand and looked both ways and slowly took the stairs and held the heavy door open for me to walk inside first and stand for a minute without him and seeing a desk, librarians, the signs saying adult books children's' books—both with arrows pointing opposite directions in case there was any confusion—one had to know oneself and make a choice. My father guided me over to children's books then left to see what he could find to read in adult books—the children's books were full of pictures and large letters, short sentences—some only a word—the world full of smiles. Then, when I was tired of being a child, I walked over to the other side to see what books my father had found. He would crouch down to how high I stood, explain the plenty of words— pick a page and tell me what it was all about and I understood because he thought I could. Now I read to find him—the year he was born and the dash that says his life ends with another year - and I am holding a book that needs another reader, another to name what father, what daughter, what books closed that held them close.

Fabric

The shirt on the floor crumpled into a human face is nothing more than what I dropped after pulling it over my head. Pulled off in the final jerk of fabric my face lies crumpled in all that it has seen I walk away from my face the resemblance I imagine and the presence of my actual face whose mouth cannot say only listen to the words cloth says or a ball in the yard or truck wheels finding a wet road to ride then sounds come in the windows sounds of ocean waves rushing in to say what they see when they hit the rocks casually tossed into the hands of sand.

Pull up a boat sit down light any fire that needs to stay lit watch it burn away what was there. The shirt on the floor winces when who steps on it will not pick it up and throw it in the washing machine full of sloshing waves and boats staying off such rough water instead float tied to the dock when the bay is calm where a fort protects from the invasion and a soldier in unfamiliar uniform watches them walk across the lowered wooden bridge welcomes them into years ago and now into the thought of then and who ran down the hill calling what remembered return to memory.

Sidewalks

It's possible to walk a long way
Over sidewalks built in 1924
Or pick another year
Return to 1943
My father writing to my mother
On the inside cover of books
Words only the young
And in love write suggesting mystery
That happened as they grew together
A mystery I did not solve
Because I was never in love enough
To pick ripe fruit off a branch
The mysterious way of being together
And not alone walking down
This sidewalk built before I was born
To walk staring at the thoughts
Of those who thought to build this here
And write one name one date one finished dream.

Real Estate

Suppose she sold the house lived elsewhere took up the lure of hearts gambled with time felt the value of the empty box what she put there to remain a moment enclosed until light again and placement. Here she begins to finish and begin. Suppose the two are different and she is different and her difference makes her suppose her new into that new place with the arched doorways at least one arch money a tender absence one arch one desire to curve. Here she curves. Loose talk on a slow train. She remembers her life. She thinks of popcorn and a houseboat.

Suppose the seas rise and she wears pearl earrings in the morning. The world is a map of places of turquoise and jade. The stone she picks up from the ground has no mouth. It speaks of the unknown. A rush of granite all the way from the pink marble front steps of her house in Atlanta to this white marble explanation of height and how to rise above initial ground voices a cigar left burning at the edge of a plate how easily it could fall off the plate the slightest movement underground how easily the plate could shake across the table find the edge and drop to the embarrassment of floor.

Suppose no one is embarrassed just hurt but let her pull herself up out of what missed the broom the crumbs dropped after sweeping how much is missed she is who gets up in the midst and stands without decoration not even silver rings keep her fingers aloft and the grip of opposable thumbs around the lid of a jar of cherry jam that will spread across toasted bread she knows that now as soon as the lid detaches and she sees the smooth ice rink top before spoon plunge and break surface upon this repetition of Eden all the way another house beginning in the middle of orchards.

I Know Because She Told Me

The desert freaks her out. The plants hold weapons, in fact her middle finger when her hands small and anxious got bit by a cactus thorn and she wouldn't stop screaming until they took her to emergency where she remembers

the white gauze. Desert sand with that look of long white passages of thorn in the finger thorn out of the finger. Time defined enough to be remembered. She does. Remember when she was young and knew nothing. The freedom from death until one day, a day for later not today, when the lizard watches *what* without naming.

Screaming Frog

I grew up on fried chicken and fish
a combo of Southern cooking
and buy whatever's cheap
I'm going to work.

It seemed quiet
except for the screams
of children at the polio hospital
across the street that had been torn
down by the time I visited
and my house and the oak tree.

Sissy MacLemore lived in the house
next door and took tadpoles home
by now they would be frogs
dead frogs just when I think
I can't be surprised
one leaps in my head and screams.

Sharp Mouth of the Cactus

Already the hills of California burn into my mouth of memory I am where I remember I am the day happening how the day wakes rises drinks sits walks lies among heavy blankets their heaviness another person in the room another reason to leave the bed to rise and walk again to the windows look out at the day and what I am of the day's rise and fall into who I am the leaving the return to daylight light where I lighten the sight of me I see look at the day's being the day that I am light lit past possible light then.

Supermoon

The last gigantic globe of light in March 1993—coming close enough to the earth—closer—wanting to ask what's it like spinning out there for you? A kiss would be perfect now, but dangerous—the allure of you, green and blue. Instead, I will shine on you until you are gone with all of them to wherever dead planets go. My friends who will look up tonight and see a large bright circle and go crazy with pleasure and past—the indifference of the moon as it is— the equal indifference of the earth—all the rocks uncaring, spinning through space, taking us for a ride—briefly beautiful and brave—we are—watching the moon come closer—the craziness it threatens, even though a man speaking to the press and representing the U.S. Naval Academy said it was no big deal—to quell the rising panic—the talk in town—the sheriff looking up at dusk—he resented what he saw as the usual oblivion to the moon. I know no one oblivious to the moon's suck and the sunshine—I promise the man tired of people ignoring the moon—the creation of endurance—enchanted and wishing—I will lean against my open back door and say hello in 2011 to the light in the sky—the particular globe coming closer, but not quite enough to make a difference to me—thrown into the rise and fall of sea tides and onto the rocks.

Words Dream from the Mouths of All the Unsaid

The ocean refuses no river no body flower from full earth
refuses no mouth opening its sounds for water to fill
with ocean songs someone sings where she is not rising
from the dead in this ground she hears familiar voices
wrapped in packages gifts for the ground she does not unwrap
her remote place that will not let her live
beyond bones beyond ash.

The lack. The demented waves of water hear the drowned
call to each other losing breath to finish together what they began.

She began when particular words named her then continued
until she reached the ocean in time for time to drown a breathing
god she swims with breaking bubbles of air remorse regret.

Words dream from the mouths of all the unsaid.

Shaking on Sunday

Earthquake. Hurricane. Impending monster. Scold of sky. Loading tobacco leaves out of the wheelbarrow into the drying barn. Blankets. A choice of shoes. Some no longer fit what the feet have become. Where they walk is my business. I keep to crosswalks. Step quickly away from snouts of trouble that arrive as silent engines and a book unread. If I answer the phone I will have to talk. Chatter. A mouth chatters into a mouthpiece. I see the same black smoke from the sugarcane fields. Word after word and someone to change the burnt out light bulbs against the ceiling with new light bulbs high up there but nothing to see inside except inside is requested ocean view something to read about not seeing the view I asked for of ocean slam and trust of wave after waves like a good long walk of footsteps of monster come to beach on a trail of seaweed moving toward an empty house whose new ceiling light bulbs shine down on down to the drowning beach under the ocean taking in swimmers who pull on the surface end of breathing.

Pasadena Freeway

The drive to Pasadena is always to the hospital even as the oranges ripen on her backyard trees even as she is told the same words over and over and believes them but does not believe them because she holds her breath until breath comes again, its coming surprises her as do the red brake lights of traffic ahead stopping suddenly. This is the thing to do. The audacity then begins again her foot off the brake and onto the gas pedal.

Yesterday she was not on the road but in the backyard watching the spring flowers push themselves into bloom watching and watching again as the woman who planted them years ago watched, now she watches for her and sees that she planted the bulbs in patches of daffodil, iris in circles to ease the straight city lot, straight as the freeway rushes her to Pasadena yet softened by tire wheels round as round gardens where she kneels to dig with her shovel the same colors of flowers in the hospital given to ease to brighten to celebrate to mourn, chosen and found near the chosen words of doctors nurses holding papers, pointing at x-rays, each word says again she cannot be well, and from her kneeling come yellow come white come pink.

Marsha

Marsha said she'd appear on Sunday and we would go to the store and buy cases of electrolyte drinks—although I remain unclear about what electrolytes actually are and why I have ended up in the ER because my electrolytes were horrendously disheveled—one time by ambulance which was a kind of public display of my failures to be a healthy human being.

The hospital allowed five liters of electrolyte liquid and then put me on a bus back to my house on another dark night—another night because nights are always dark so it is not necessary to repeat the obvious—unless the lights are turned on yet still there's that suggestion in the background that now is night and you had better be either dancing or sleeping.

Wild Mustard

The wild mustard in California sun yellow mustard yellow spice
filling a jar then spread across bread eaten believed to taste good
smear left on napkins on a table not in California of course I am
remembering the world as it was much to remember many
attempts to forget then the almond orchards of white bloom
beautiful among the letters of the alphabet Cuba also beginning
with that half-moon rising over the trees there caught in my name
then all that comes with bloom butterflies birds yellow butter
spread as a blanket over what needs now to be warm growing
colder unless summer comes wildfires burn in the hills reach into
windows I leave again always leaving this chance to see Castro in
a blue jacket and baseball cap sits in a car reaching out to shake
the hands of tourists from Venezuela what did it all mean except
that his name begins with that half-moon whose light is the curve
of a harbor the boats at the dock the world tied up ready to sail
away always leaving every four years running through wild
mustard until I am no longer anywhere I recognize who sold my
world short did not shake my hand quarreled no longer able to
love this disappearance of yellow the failure of words to raise
what flag.

Valentine Island

If a tomato is a starfish then I am macaroni in cheese sauce quick in the mouth, if not this time I appear ready for transport into the airport of everywhere at once and translating at the same time an understanding. The sun umbrella is down and down on the lips of the wooden bench only branches to consider or the tasty pretense of paper trash in trucks careening up and down the street in front of the house where I listen to the city buses stop and gather and expel human riders this time *son montuno* almost sun that means dance sounds through rooms in time to music where only sound matters in the only existence of sound enough to play meaning through the unsung known of words, another instrument strums the back of my throat and this face smiling enough to show teeth as I will when I am in Cuba on Valentine's Day give myself an entire island to love to say I love you to the dead left behind the swallowed taste of empty metal.

Yankaway

In Osceola, Arkansas live the Yankaway
family: Ruthie Mae, Sammy, and Lerotha.
Ruthie Mae and Sammy live in the same
house on Jefferson while Lerotha
moved to E. Village. I don't know
any of them, know only of them from
the smallest phone book that I've seen
in the States. I brought the phone book
home after being forced by a tornado
to stop in Osceola at a motel.

This isn't about small town friendliness.
They weren't friendly. The waitress
in the motel restaurant didn't
smile at me until after I'd had four beers.

This is about what kind of woman
would drive four days for two
days of sex: a good two days mostly
because they were the first such
two days all year and it was already
the end of October.

Whore, Driving

Touching her fear, I am like
that dumb whore who let
three cars pull out in front
of her car at the Safeway parking lot
because she was in no hurry
to go anywhere and was actually just
trying to be kind, but being
kind to anyone means someone
will call you dumb and a whore
and aren't we all until we are
kind to death and let it take us
on a white-sheeted bed
the tumble under a blue blanket
the sex good enough to kill us.

This Morning, Listening from Her Bed

A motorcycle
revs down the street:
so it isn't raining

and the skies
call for a walk

around her
backyard: earth
swallows winter's

frozen ground
fled from the mountains

of firs that are here
with her this body
of minding

mind reminding.
She thinks
of motorcycles

and leather's protection:
if a bike and body fall

toward afternoon
then the sun is high

with plans to set due west
when they walk home
in darkness.

Love Seat for Sale—$75 OBO

The beige boat parked outside says I'm supposed to leave by water
says the seas wait for me to finger their waves, jump into the air,
those are rivers and the thick orange of salmon leap
further than a hook and line can catch or not further and caught
to sit on the far side of this couch, this shortened version of a
relationship implied by the love tacked in front of it.

What do the fish say aside from talking endlessly about water and
the bears that come to snatch them out and yum another tasty
critter eaten out of view. I'm sitting on the near side by the
window and don't even own this piece of pie, this furniture, only
saw it for sale and imagine the happiness of the couple as they buy
the hope that goes with it all those fish dinners the smell fills the
house and on the side, a baked potato.

Boat Trip

She's on the river in the rain trying to drown all her pain thinking
country western having spent time on Texas prairies she's
authentic staring at river water looping from shore to shore
sometimes a branch of both tree and river a smaller uncut vein
to her right disappearing into never solved mystery what's down
that road she will never know but will think about as she is now
avoiding a windy outside deck where freedom would blow her
around knowing that she stays inside and her gaze fishes the
river.

Here come the fish one in pieces on her plate another always
going for a swim and sometimes breathing rain water but today
never letting go of the slippery metal bannister going to the top
deck and the wind riding her toward chairs where other people
stare and cower in a community of boat and water and
remember the bluebonnets and weed growing by the lake until
she joyfully recognized it and pulled it out and smoked it
anticipating a revival into swimming head above water
another current, another fin.

An Obsession with Umbrellas

Useful in the rain until the weather becomes provocatively windy then close quickly before it blows into pieces what protects you. Even if you make it home or wherever you are going water drips on the floor before you have time to shake it once, twice, your best intentions thwarted. Two people cannot stand under one umbrella and not at least get wet unless they stand very close, fall in love, then open another umbrella the way a heart opens when love rains down even sideways and those puddles full of a future of evaporation when it is dry out and you do not need an umbrella but still you hear rain. Drops splash into your mouth. For a second you stick out your tongue taste heaven become an angel live to talk about it, the sudden way what thought opens into you there. You are dry walking on the inside of a life you do not understand no matter how deeply you think about not being splashed you are splashed not the worst thing just water reminding you that the umbrella needs to keep moving since the rain keeps moving. You adjust the angle of the umbrella. You are with the clouds. The heavy rain reminds you that the clouds are not yours to care about, but it is heavenly to think that they care about you involved in the art of keeping dry staying dry if it weren't for this wind forcing you into the water where you breathe always in love.

Leaving Portland

She finds a good bar and a dope dealer.

She takes the 15 downtown and out to Flanders
where she sees a therapist about something become nothing.
She gets her hair done at Blu pronounced as *blue*
or *blew* until her lips go purple but she's happy in the wind.

She's no longer the stranger in town,
"the stranger who gets stranger by the hour"
to quote some poet whose name she forgets.

Nothing takes over. It slams her back and forth.
Awakens the sadness caught sleeping.

A couple of bus drivers wave at her, she walks past
with her small dog who finally knows the way (doesn't matter).

Soon she'll be moving again across well-defined state lines
and is certain to be sober
around an unused pack of rolling papers,
her hair torn from her mind (never mind),
but she's going—the car itches in the driveway
and she scratches until she bleeds blue.

Flight Plan

The over story is always the sky.

Perhaps you are on a plane and I watch you.

and the world clears the road

of fallen branches and bullets until again

a guitar accompanies a voice on the rocky

hills of ruins, see, I took a photograph

you are the little one beside the house

before it too disappeared.

Talented love would be a love for birds.

Their startle and fly away on various wings

feathered and lousy with lice.

Oregon grape is the understory in dank fir forests

where unknown children walk carrying breadcrumbs,

look for candy and the delicious hug of a witch

or is that another story

then a green barrel full of heavy wet leaves

almost at the curb for Monday morning,

(pick up right at 6)

So no slacking. Tell a story. Live a lie.

Plane Going Down

The expected long ride
cut short
was it the left wing dipping
toward the water
as if needing a drink now
that made her look
know what could
have been said
before she left forever
in the speed of suddenly
down into ocean water
where thinking about it
in the brevity of life left
she swims to safety
breaking apart
before she can take
her first stroke
arms reaching out anyway
to hold the crash
that ends her flight
not flying until landing
correctly and not the long walk
to luggage and continuation.

The Red Suitcase

The body in the red suitcase only wanted to travel

and wheel the red suitcase out to the tarmac

board the plane and stare out the window

that seemed inadequate for the job of staring

instead she met a man who killed her

and left her by the side of the road

in a red suitcase a color learned from blood

drained from her folded body

her face where she packed sweaters

to be warm in winter had they never met.

Heart Break

Someone drops a glass of red
wine in the kitchen.
She studies it. She is also on the floor.
Her gaze focuses
on the glacial broken glass
the liquid congealing into a spill
over linoleum. The floor apparently
not level but hills and valleys
lit rooms of other lives
or at least pools of water
after heavy rain
and her without a raincoat
an umbrella, boots.

The mud from her walk outside, inside.
She reaches for a piece of glass
holds it like home—the house the trees
the friendly neighbors
turn their porch lights on at night
that last look out
the windows before bed.
She can't sleep on the floor
someone has to sweep up
it might as well be her.

A bottle steady on the counter
she reaches for another glass fills it
and drinks a long time thirsty.
The neighbors wave.

Rough

The river shatters through with the indifference of glass that can never care as you care, yet there are bridges. You want to leave and you just got here where the camellias bloomed and are dropping blossoms as another bud opens a quick mouth against air and you breathe if only to wait and see your next breath appear in whatever guise keeps you breathing life invited wonder of why/why not eyes remarkable in the mirror's seduction of self and time while another mark appears on your calendar face, the faces of your friends turn into faces living lives demanding more than the wisdom of trees. Then you again the keeper of your soul, that soul—the who of you—digs into the ground.

Thunder

The dogs bark. The gods are angry say those who believe in gods—the gods are always angry— or out in the back alley by the dumpster—smoking a cigarette—or making themselves terribly wealthy—which I have successfully avoided doing—but the thunder still pounds their various drums in the clouds. I watch for rain from my bedroom window—try to calm the dogs—the next-door neighbor managed to prune her lilac bush into a few clipped branches—I wonder about spring—whether that lilac is too broken to receive it—wonder whether I am too broken to take next spring into my awareness of more thunder. I let the rush of birds rise and settle.

The weeds of life overtake my yard—the earth in the middle of a year—I go along—but see autumn leaves—my mother's favorite song—want to mark the time as changed—then rush me past those flowers that used to stop me—long enough to say beautiful—among all this truth—the insertion of beauty into the monologue of truth—asserting appearance—not reality—the reality of beauty is too quick to mention—easy to love—love uneasy around that older look I see in the mirror before I walk outside—search for gods.

Smudge

There are words to be deleted and the songs of others or the missing whose anticipated shapes fill with smoke and I am embracing them until the smoke alarm goes off a bird gone mad in a wingless fall letting me know that I fall also into thinking turned to ice suddenly easy to slip into opening the door to let cold air in and quiet what screams louder than joyful sounds long silenced the space empty as a cup I put on the counter round mouth says oh fill me and drink otherwise go thirsty dry out laundry in the sun an empty shirt crucified wet down the buttons one dropped to the ground in prayer.

Golden

Another unanswered question. Somewhere in the world. A map of many streets all in different cities. Not enough to unknow. The woman next door makes that noise with her garbage cans. The early morning truck. The late morning truck. Impossible sleep. Either cold or hot. Unable to identify myself during the photographs of constant unheard noise. My silence within your silence. Where are you? Every morning is another tear to swallow. I drink black coffee and salty ocean water. This island rises out of water. I am entire. No. Apart. Far. Will we get together later? Have you left forever and only the marketplace sells you as an idea a good idea missing a body without the space you left to travel now one traveler gone another lost in the loss. The untied knot. Rope falls to ground rising into dust and the animal wanders away. I'll go alone and then we'll go together. As if all that time together never was the proof of grief proving again again again. More clouds. More water. Your empty bowl. I drink.

Red Curtains

Virginia Woolf liked red curtains.
I think that is a fact.

Another fact: I sit in a living room
in Portland, Oregon with red
curtains on the windows.
I have pulled the curtains open
and can see the house
across the street.
This is more than one fact.

It is tough to separate fact from truth.

A light is on in the living room
inside the house across the street.
We are awake together, but apart.
The river is a city bus ride away.
Virginia Woolf walked to her river,
walked quickly, walked into the river
until the stones she carried pulled her down.

The red curtains fall from ceiling to floor.

They are heavier than blood.
Neither bright nor cheerful, they just are
as I am with my two dogs in this blue house
that is not blue sky and sun,
but could be water and drowning.

The Ceiling

And over there
are the pencils
annoyed and terrible,
the light beside them
shines around shadows
dropped on the table
over the book too dark
to read further
about the woman
staring at ceilings
where small planes land
and shake the house,
so leave her there,
flat land to stare into,
assumptions
and the gold of fools
looking up
and swallowing
something liquid,
to drink the lake
where she swims
in circles so small,
so small the end
of her tongue
glistens. Often she
will not see the ceiling,
but the floor is dry and
the sky is hidden.

Stairscape

She collects stairs. They either climb or descend sometimes both up and down at the same time life works that way such confusion of loss and gain or no confusion just a clarity of one or the other when moments gather to cut her gut or gather as flowers gather into a bouquet tossed intentionally her way that she catches before walking up the marble stairs the building gone but the stairs available to climb not as high as she'd like but high enough for her rough rose in the road dropped down for her footsteps to do their rising again the great height the banister chokes in her grip with each conquered stair glory of travel of leave and arrive another mind shift mountain an entire range.

Maybe she sits on the top stair. Stares out at the horizon cusped at the edge of any stair. The rise and fall of sun's steps of footsteps of mind filled moon great white bouncing ball thrown back and forth between gods and star lift and shine into shapes in place for the while of sight of stars wrapped around her temporary heart the stairs winding round her visit. Her furniture a collection of chairs some rocking some sitting by a window one pulled up to a table and a basket of apples and trees her memory of dangle and drop a chair pulled up to a desk her books across the room on shelves stair struck sentences rise the fall when every step feels its stair of only the climbing and a wish rising yes rising.

First It Was Hot and Then It Was Dark

All this time trying hard to be alive,
the earth famously gone. Nothing to think
because no one was thinking.

First it was hot and then it was dark.
She took off her sweater, turned on a light,
thought past the point of thinking.

Was there ever such a world repeated,
the entire place entirely too interesting
and entirely too forgotten?

The Chicken and the Cave

Oh here in the dark underground
beside the rock wall where
fish gurgle and wince
flash their fins against wave
after wave of water splash
of moon breath into earth's
caves filling with swim
and glimmer and the flames
burn everything that is not rock
burn the sad searching hen
whose feathers windmill
oh here in small air.

Entry

As far as words go, the door is open:
space is immeasurably empty full of old light
and time measures the prolific nameless:
the casual some in photographs
or before, the weight of which is unknown unless:
go back a few years, the plastic slide rule
left in the top desk drawer becomes usable again,
then drink one glass of wine in celebration
and sputter as the cellular motors of old brains sputter
perfectly yet afraid in museums:
their drivers wear jackets,
stand unmoving in corners
and never return to comprehend their loss.

Morning Eggs

She drinks another cup of coffee at the kitchen table looking out
the window over the path to the chickens who need to lay another
dozen eggs for her to deliver them out in cartons to her customers
in the city who dream of owning a farm and carrying a basket of
herbs and wearing overalls over linen shirts covered in a botanical
print.

She thinks about the barn slap a coat of paint on it hay stored in
bundles and the beautiful horses all at a gallop outside in the
round green pasture the field beyond then a line of trees she'd be
more specific but a dream only goes so far someone with a
hammer across the road the clouds have the quiet of mud then
rain on her run to get new eggs into her basket.

Scrambled poached sunny side soft boiled hard life on a farm this
living off the land that she decided to begin with 30 packs of
vegetable seeds all of them struggled except for the carrots
she mashed with brown sugar though still they crunched orange
icicles during frozen weather but summer coming now and the
first egg delivery keeps an open tab on time.

Weathervane

The usual pointing in various directions depending on the wind
and its ways the roads the wind takes traveling from one side to
another of mountains of water of prairie covered today in enough
wildflowers to be in a book naming them bluebonnet and other
names I forget because that book is packed in a box soon to be
lifted into a truck whose concealing metal sides name the
company and what it does to transport what must come along
wrapped in bubble wrap those precise air bubbles I pop when
packing my pop's books his translations of what he turned into
hesitant English refusing laughter refusing his name his history
the insect at the hospital window lifting into the wind then
reappearance someone bouncing a small ball against the window
in a room where I lost an earring and heard him try to lecture me
one more time this time about the different kinds of ice the ice in
his glass disappearing into water nobody thirsty I agreed with him
about everything until he did not remember me one less daughter
one less dad my dad who knew the June bug the wind silent and
near enough to hear the canyon where *easy does it* he might say
the drop far to the ground where maybe a yellow flower this time
short of bloom blooming on desert sands blown angry against hills
become a reason for hills that the truck struggles up keeps in low
gear makes it oh joyful recognition until boxes settle into the new
place and unpacked I find the book of wildflowers that dance in
wind the weathervane points out south to north the decoration of
rusted rooster crowing surely pecks at seed.

Yellow Birds

Yellow birds fill the yard with yellow
and that forsythia of course about to bloom yellow
and those yellow roses that were a bad mistake,
not here or now, but years ago she held them
at her wedding, everything already wrong,
but she, sure of her power, kept on with the vows,
until she learned to promise nothing to herself,
or to others and not to believe their promises.

She began to fear she would never be loved
that the walk to the front door would be back
and forth and the groceries always for her,
let the yellow stay outside, she looks for colors
that will blush on her table to fill an empty
vase with another color another color another.

My Aunt and the Parrot

My aunt who never married had a parrot from the age of 17
the parrot lived 47 years longer than all my dogs put together
never barked only spoke of good times laid no eggs laughed
interrupting any serious conversation while the green laundry
hung out to dry never dried in the continuous rain and regretted
any squish of mud an inability to breathe while nestled
even as a root against it to grow what began long ago
to be that bird and the woman beside that bird
once she felt she flew but it was the dreaming bird dreaming.

Cowgirl

This rodeo haunts me with the limited reach

of my left arm no more rope tricks

twirl and spin a memory

in the center of the ring where

my head shakes out stars of salt

seasoning a night sky and the calling ground

prints my name with kicked stones.

Acupuncture

The sweet dreams of needles plunged into meridian points that connect to the earth and stars giving away that quiver of *qi* up your arms into the cavern where a heart used to be and actually still is but the cave seems larger with steep walls climbing higher than the sky although to pierce a necessary point while you lie on the table and feel the plunge.

The plant in your bedroom has big leaves and an arrogant attitude. Objects abound. The book on shoes you bought because you had to, because you did not buy it before and thought about it and felt it as loss, suddenly now the book reappears and that loss can be filled perfectly. Unlike. Unlike.

How much needs to be explained about loss remaining lost? The earth as burial for secrets, the stories never told and only one person knows and will not say but asks for the needles to dream and break the narration.

While Planting Fruit Trees

Where are the unnecessary angels who stand panicked and unbidden? Is it another Sunday with no oranges? Although three bananas lie browning in a blue bowl not anything else but a blue bowl at the moment. The words are dizzy with love and think lake then everything changes as it just did now with a boat appearing and the lost faces of fish and other relatives impressed with their new surroundings. Sudden lake on a kitchen counter? But the sink sits where the memory is of a frog underwater then rising to meditate on a pad until its larynx puffs and warbles as that crow warbles in my backyard that is still my backyard and I own the rising grass.

Real or imagined dahlias at the end of August. Is it still possible to love? The bloom of such a word. Such a thought while standing in the kitchen and looking at a magazine making expensive suggestions. A suggestion about flowers: find a lavender farm on the other side of Mount Hood. Pick a bouquet. Flowers everywhere on front doorknobs come May first remember May Day and the paper baskets that Jill and I filled with flowers from our Berkeley yards and hung on front doors because that was life then and is now if I think of the tender air.

Who opens the door every morning to walk out away from the lake the docked boat a romance and then another? On dry land other flowers bloom the pink wild roses the orange tree but this tree is not on this property but somewhere in Southern California grow intense oranges easy to peel walk outside pick one eat it doesn't get better than that, although to know that and not move away, not leave the loved, but keep loving the presence, only later as in now I plant a cherry tree a yellow apple an Asian pear to replicate another in this chilly rush of water climate where it will be dry and hot over the next few days so early morning is best. Hear the wings? The pull of wings? Jesus Christ. Amen.

Hello

She's unpacking now and doing okay thanks for asking.

Never enough bubble wrap for what she decides is enough glass.

But you know how it goes: the inevitability of glass

The breaking of here comes another cup smack against the sink.

At least all the sharp edges are gathered in one place.

She's fine with a paper towel until that always-lurking edge.

Gets her. Blood on her hands again with that same vivacity

of the round red flower rug she buys today at the thrift store

because she is nothing if not

thrifty except for the last two months all those holidays.

She really likes the crimson to pink to yellow to the center

of every flower on her 1944 oak floor under the window

that faces the street and needs a curtain

another lace curtain from the box marked curtains

and that is true such a relief.

Usually she lights a cigarette and stares into the street.

Roads

They bring themselves to us or we go there or keep going until we are farther away than mere far away we are gone or tired of going so at a motel and eat bad coleslaw in the attached café all day we have been out looking but for what and the noise at 3AM is not what we want so away we leave on a fast road highway life where the rest stops seem to be planted with berry brambles that take their ramble all over the unarmed dry ground and against just my ankle because you have left us taking the ginger candy with you chewing it until that cavity in your mouth grows far and wide you turn inside out climb the tender trail on the east side stop before going drink from your water bottle until the pit in your tooth floods fills with water grasses nervous dreams and here you are in a photograph years later.

Someone tells the road outside where to go or it tells us and it goes wanting to be there instead of here where nearness grates with a long ago sound of chalk on chalkboard we held our ears until we were deaf from holding and did not hear the splash of the swimmer rising for breath out of the water then falling back into the water the dolphin uncaught sings about freedom while the busy water stands arms akimbo until there is no reason not to leave your mouth and its talking shelf of books Ophelia floats by taking a road of water a boat that sinks but here's one in full sail this windy journey of going going gone wait I think you try to make a U-turn before you're flattened by a truck rise and eat a traveling cloud.

Midnight Bus

There it is again. I watch it sometimes stop sometimes not and I am standing in the kitchen watching it be a bus that passes my house at midnight. I am awake having taken to watching late-night movies—often there is an irresistible moon—impossible to resist light during midnight with a moon shining—I look up take in the light I see, think it shines for me, think it knows my name and loves that I am standing here spoon in one hand the other hand empty—the spoon moon-shaped ready to scoop from the round carton of vanilla yogurt—my troubled tongue rolls in its cave—my eyes see far enough away—everything is full moon. Easy to see the bus pass under all that has been thrown into the sky. We shine.

The Strange Mistakes of Fish

Blue dreams swimming in my friend's fish tank
the five that I must feed for a day and turn on the light
so they see the water as much as they feel
the water in the dark now lit with daydreams
lucky unknowing dreams swimming from edge to edge
flicking their tails wishing for something to happen
other than this constant swimming toward glass
a strange mistake familiar this reaching
too far away where even a glance is dangerous
and the water dreamt of suddenly becomes air.

McKenna

The woman across the street packs her bull horn
into a soft-sided suitcase in preparation
for a drive across country to Virginia
on 40 not going through the deep south
because her car has Oregon plates
and she's tattooed and carrying cannabis
but it's a free country and she's driven on one road
or another across country going on 15 times
make up your mind pick west or east
and drive that way here are some hard candies for the trip
nothing much else to do about a friend's leaving
along a route I drove myself in an 1984 red Camaro
with 3 narrow gold stripes under the windows
and the car drove well until the engine fell out
and onto the street and ground to a halt
defeated by east coast underbody rust.

I bought a square and serious white Honda
that I confused with other white Hondas
and tried to open doors that were not mine
until whatever caught my eye on the back seat
was not my sweater and my key did not fit
did not unlock did not have me sitting down
having the key turn on the engine and that sound
is my friend leaving and taking with her a small dog
hard candy and her bull horn quiet about the loud road ahead.

First Line

I forgot the first line—it was strong and taut—strung between two trees—covered in clothespins and, at times, birds—a bad idea perhaps to hang a line near birds—envision an empty white shirt with the wind shaping it with wind's breath—making sense of clothes—the way they look like a body—the way a body suddenly needs new clothes—suddenly because the world turns happy or because only a white shirt will do on the plane flying to her loss and I cannot wear black all the time these days and nights, in fact I have three closets and one is filled with my black clothes— the crying closet—dark when the door opens—clothes difficult to tell apart, but ready for the inevitable news of the end of a story—all the other times life almost ended, but for the facts that the truck did not hit hard enough or she was next but the soldiers heard the lunch bell and were hungry enough to leave her standing against the wall or suddenly the medication takes while the leaves and fever turn—the tree bends but stands—old at the corner of the yard that this autumn has orange berries among the branches empty all summer of leaves—the clothesline tugging at it— wanting nothing of life, but to hold clothes or birds would give it reason just as well—but I have lost the line that last night began the poem—the clothes lie on the ground where I have thrown them—I miss her miss her and feel again that I lean against loneliness and wear an empty shirt—as someone readies to leave and I open the closet door to see the clothes and nothing else— nothing—the everything of nothing come again for birds and their inevitable flight.

ABOUT THE AUTHOR

 **Carol Ellis** is a poet living in Portland, Oregon. She's been around the academic block with her Ph.D. in English from the University of Iowa (her dissertation was about the poet James Wright) and her Masters of English and Creative Writing from San Francisco State, where she studied with Robert Creeley, and Ed Dorn. Carol is the author of two chapbooks: *HELLO* (Two Plum Press, 2018), and *I Want a Job* (Finishing Line Press, 2014). Her poems and essays are published in anthologies and journals including ZYZZYVA, Comstock Review, The Cincinnati Review, Saranac Review, and Cider Press Review. Carol has taught at Saginaw Valley State University, University of Redlands, California State University at San Bernardino, Claremont Graduate University (where she directed the graduate writing program), University of California at Merced, and at The Attic in Portland. In 2015, Carol spent time in Cuba writing a book and giving readings.

ABOUT PACIFIC COAST POETRY SERIES

The Pacific Coast Poetry Series, an imprint of Beyond Baroque Books, was founded by poet Henry Morro in 2013, together with co-editor Suzanne Lummis and associate editor Liz Camfiord.

The Pacific Coast Poetry Series has a special interest in the American West, but is open to poets nationwide. We favor accomplished poetry that's both lucid and smart, poetry that might surprise the reader through its wit or through its depth of feeling.

Our first publication, *Wide Awake: Poets of Los Angeles and Beyond*, was cited by The Los Angeles Times as one of the Best Books of 2015. In 2017, we published *Our Foreigner* by the noted Northwest Coast poet, Nance Van Winckel. Molly Bendall, in her review for Tupelo Quarterly, praised Van Winckel's "wisecracking and shifty voice," and the way she "holds us captive even as she might unexpectedly jump the tracks."

In 2018, *In Order of Disappearance* by Carine Topal became the third book in the Pacific Coast Poetry Series and was lauded by Dorothy Barresi as a "breathtaking meditation on death, injustice, and the lyric memory's power to name what survives when everything has been stripped away."

Lost and Local by Carol Ellis is Pacific Coast Poetry Series' fourth publication.

Pacific Coast Poetry Series would like to thank the Lawrence Lipton Trust for its generous support.

ABOUT LAWRENCE LIPTON

Lawrence Lipton was born in Poland, 1903, and in the 30s through the 60s established himself as a novelist, journalist and poet, first in Chicago and later in Los Angeles. In Chicago he mingled with the noted writers and literati, Carl Sandburg, Ben Hecht, and Harriet Monroe, editor of the famed literary magazine, Poetry.

In addition to his literary novels *Brother, the Laugh is Bitter* and *Secret Battle,* Lipton also wrote mystery novels. His work appeared in newspapers, literary journals and magazines including The Jewish Daily Forward, The Quarterly Review of Literature and The Atlantic Monthly. He published a poetry collection, *Rainbow at Midnight.*

Lipton's *The Holy Barbarians*, published in 1959, explored the impact of the "Beats" upon the society of that day. In his analysis Lipton noted, "When the barbarians appear on the frontiers of a civilization it is a sign of a crisis in that civilization. If the barbarians come, not with weapons of war but with the songs and ikons of peace, it is a sign that the crisis is one of a spiritual nature. In either case the crisis is never welcomed by the entrenched beneficiaries of the status quo. In the case of the holy barbarians it is not an enemy invasion threatening the gates, it is 'a change felt in the rhythm of events' that signals one of those 'cyclic turns' which the poet Robinson Jeffers has written about."

Lipton's son, James Lipton, won wide fame as the executive producer, writer and host of the renowned Bravo series *Inside the Actors Studio.*

Lawrence Lipton died in Los Angeles in 1975. The Lawrence Lipton Trust was created by his widow to support poets.

ABOUT BEYOND BAROQUE BOOKS

The Beyond Baroque Foundation began in 1968 as an avant-garde poetry magazine called *Beyond Baroque*. Editor, publisher and founder George Drury Smith created the Beyond Baroque press in order to publish emerging, over-looked, as well as established, poets — especially those from Los Angeles. The Foundation began issuing perfect bound books and chapbooks in 1971. Titles include *Building Some Changes*, the first book from Los Angeles' first Poet Laureate, Eloise Klein Healy, Maxine Chernoff's first collection, *Vegetable Emergency* as well as K. Curtis Lyle's *15 Predestination Weather Reports*. Beyond Baroque, through its various publications, also published works by Dennis Cooper, Amy Gerstler, Bill Mohr, Harry Northup, Holly Prado, and Wanda Coleman to name a few. The Foundation's current press, Beyond Baroque Books, was launched in 1998 by Fred Dewey. It has published numerous books and several magazines featuring works by Jean-Luc Godard, Jack Hirschman, Diane di Prima, David Meltzer, Puma Perl and more. Beyond Baroque Books continues to unearth cult rarities as well as collections by noted performance poets, educators, and cultural leaders. Pacific Coast Poetry Series is an imprint of Beyond Baroque Books.

ABOUT BEYOND BAROQUE

Based in the original City Hall building in Venice, California, Beyond Baroque celebrated its 50th anniversary in 2018 as one of the United States' leading independent Literary Arts Centers, dedicated to expanding the public's knowledge of poetry, literature and art through cultural events and community interaction. The building also houses The Mike Kelley Gallery and a bookstore, The Scott Wannberg Bookstore and Poetry Lounge, which stocks an extensive collection of new poetry as well as an archive of more than 40,000 books, including small press and limited-edition publications, chronicling the history of poetry movements in Los Angeles and beyond. Since its founding in 1968 as a magazine by George Drury Smith, Beyond Baroque has played muse to the Venice Beats, the burgeoning Punk movement and visiting scholars.

Beyond Baroque's mission is to advance the literary arts; to provide a challenging program of events which promotes new work and diversity; to foster the exchange of ideas and the nurturing of writers through readings, workshops, books sales, publication, access to archived material and performance space; to encourage collaboration and cross-fertilization between writers and artists in multiple disciplines and to use the literary arts as a foundation for increasing education and literacy in our community and among our youth.

Made in the USA
Lexington, KY
04 December 2019